Sch

Clockwise

First published in Great Britain in 1999 by Macdonald Young Books

Macdonald Young Books,
an imprint of Wayland Publishers Ltd
61 Western Road
Hove, East Sussex
BN3 1JD

Commissioning Editor: Dereen Taylor
Editor: Lisa Edwards
Designer: Rebecca Elgar
Language Consultant: Dr Carol Ballard
Creature Consultant: Stephen Savage

A CIP catalogue for this book is available from the British Library
Printed and bound in Portugal by Edições ASA

ISBN 0 7500 2665 0

Clockwise

Sam Godwin

Illustrated by
Anthony Lewis

MACDONALD YOUNG BOOKS

Tick...tick...tick.
Time is ticking away.

We use the word **time** all the time.

But how do we measure time?

The smallest unit of time you can measure on a clock is a second.

In 1 second, a hummingbird flaps its wings 78 times.

That gives us just enough time to jump in the air once!

The second hand measures seconds.
It moves forward 1 mark every second.

Penguin feeding

time: 1.30pm

A watch like this one
is a clock you wear
on your wrist.

You can see the seconds marked
around the edge of the clock.
There are 60 of them.

Sixty seconds make one minute.

In 1 minute, a cheetah can run 4 times round a race track.

Wow!

The minute hand measures minutes.
It moves forward 1 mark every minute.

But you'd still be tying the laces on your running shoes.

The marks around the edge
of the clock measure minutes
as well as seconds.

In 1 hour the minute hand moves
once round the clock.

At the same time, the hour hand moves
forward from 1 number to the next.
The numbers count the hours.

13

There are 5 minute marks
between each number.

You should eat
your greens too.

Count them and you will
find out how many minutes
past the hour it is.

15

Twenty-four hours make one day.

In 1 day, a lion can eat enough meat to make 140 burgers and rests for 20 hours.

16

In 1 day the hour hand goes round the clock twice.

In 1 day we go to school, play with our friends and sleep for several hours.

It measures 12 hours twice.
That makes 24 hours.

17

You can see the days of the week marked
on a diary or a calendar.
Each day has its own name.

MONDAY

TUESDAY

WEDNESDAY

THURSDAY

FRIDAY

SATURDAY

SUNDAY

Thirty or thirty-one days make one month.

In 1 month, a caterpillar changes into a butterfly.

In the same time, your hair grows 1 centimetre longer.

Each month has a different name. You can see them on this calendar. Some months have 30 days, others have 31 days. February usually has 28 days but every 4 years it has 29.

JANUARY

M	T	W	T	F	S	S
	1	2	3	4	5	
6	7	8	9	10	11	12
13	14	15	16	17	18	19
20	21	22	23	24	25	26
27	28	29	30	31		

FEBRUARY

M	T	W	T	F	S	S
				1	2	
3	4	5	6	7	8	9
10	11	12	13	14	15	16
17	18	19	20	21	22	23
24	25	26	27	28		

MARCH

M	T	W	T	F	S	S
				1	2	
3	4	5	6	7	8	9
10	11	12	13	14	15	16
17	18	19	20	21	22	23
24	25	26	27	28	29	30
31						

APRIL

M	T	W	T	F	S	S
	1	2	3	4	5	6
7	8	9	10	11	12	13
14	15	16	17	18	19	20
21	22	23	24	25	26	27
28	29	30				

MAY

M	T	W	T	F	S	S
	1	2	3	4		
5	6	7	8	9	10	11
12	13	14	15	16	17	18
19	20	21	22	23	24	25
26	27	28	29	30	31	

JUNE

M	T	W	T	F	S	S
					1	
2	3	4	5	6	7	8
9	10	11	12	13	14	15
16	17	18	19	20	21	22
23	24	25	26	27	28	29
30						

JULY

M	T	W	T	F	S	S
1	2	3	4	5	6	
7	8	9	10	11	12	13
14	15	16	17	18	19	20
21	22	23	24	25	26	27
28	29	30	31			

AUGUST

M	T	W	T	F	S	S
				1	2	3
4	5	6	7	8	9	10
11	12	13	14	15	16	17
18	19	20	21	22	23	24
25	26	27	28	29	30	31

SEPTEMBER

M	T	W	T	F	S	S
1	2	3	4	5	6	7
8	9	10	11	12	13	14
15	16	17	18	19	20	21
22	23	24	25	26	27	28
29	30					

OCTOBER

M	T	W	T	F	S	S
	1	2	3	4	5	
6	7	8	9	10	11	12
13	14	15	16	17	18	19
20	21	22	23	24	25	26
27	28	29	30	31		

NOVEMBER

M	T	W	T	F	S	S
				1	2	
3	4	5	6	7	8	9
10	11	12	13	14	15	16
17	18	19	20	21	22	23
24	25	26	27	28	29	30

DECEMBER

M	T	W	T	F	S	S
1	2	3	4	5	6	7
8	9	10	11	12	13	14
15	16	17	18	19	20	21
22	23	24	25	26	27	28
29	30	31				

Twelve months make one year.

In 1 year, a baby giraffe grows about 100 centimetres or 1 metre.

You grow about 6 centimetres taller.

Every year is given a number. This helps people remember when things happened.

If you put the name
and number of a day

THURSDAY 14

next to the name
of a month

AUGUST

and the number
of a year

1997

you get a date

THURSDAY, 14 AUGUST 1997

Do you know your own date of birth?

Ten centuries make one millenium.

At the end of a millenium, people celebrate.

It's time to have fun!

27

Look at the time!

A sun dial is a very old kind of stone clock. You can tell what time it is by checking where the sun's shadow falls. The time on this sun dial is 3 o' clock.

▼

▲

A grandfather clock has a part called a pendulum. It swings backwards and forwards to show that the clock is working properly. It makes a loud ticking sound as well.

An alarm clock wakes you up in the morning. Some alarm clocks have a loud ring or buzzer. Others have a radio.

You wear a wristwatch on a strap around your wrist. You can tell the time wherever you are.

An hour glass measures time by letting sand slip from the top part of it to the lower part.

GLOSSARY

DAY
A length of time lasting 24 hours. Part of a day is in darkness and part in daylight.

MONTH
A length of time made up of 30 or 31 days. One month, February, is different. It has 28 days, and every four years it has 29 days. There are 12 months in one year.

UNIT
A fixed amount of something. For example, the second is a unit of time.

HOUR
A length of time made up of 60 minutes. There are 24 hours in one day.

SECOND
A very short length of time. There are 60 seconds in one minute.

WEEK
A length of time made up of 7 days.

MINUTE
A short length of time made up of 60 seconds. There are 60 minutes in one hour.

TIME
We know that time passes by the way days and nights repeat themselves or the movement of the hands on a clock. We measure time by using units such as seconds, minutes and hours.

YEAR
A length of time made up of 12 months, or 52 weeks, or 365 days.

OTHER M.Y.Bees FOR YOU TO ENJOY:

The Earth is like a Roundabout – a first look
at night and day
Claire Llewellyn
Illustrated by Anthony Lewis
ISBN: 07500 2644 8

My Amazing Journey – a first look
at where babies come from
Pat Thomas
Illustrated by Lesley Harker
ISBN: 07500 2573 5

My Family's Changing – a first look
at family break-up
Pat Thomas
Illustrated by Lesley Harker
ISBN: 07500 2571 9

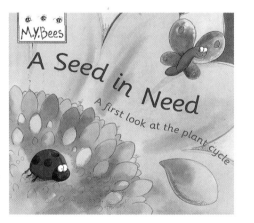

The Trouble with Tadpoles – a
first look at the life cycle of a frog
Sam Godwin
Illustrated by Simone Abel
ISBN: 07500 2652 9

The Case of the Missing Caterpillar – a first look at
the life cycle of a butterfly
Sam Godwin
Illustrated by Simone Abel
ISBN: 07500 2651 0

A Seed in Need – a first look
at the plant cycle
Sam Godwin
Illustrated by Simone Abel
ISBN: 07500 2496 8

All these books and many more can be purchased from your local bookseller. For more information, write to:

The Sales Department   Macdonald Young Books   61 Western Road   Hove   BN3 1JD